I0883717

EDGE BOOKS

DOGS ON THE JOB

MILITARY DOGS

by Tammy Gagne

Consultant:
Ronald L. Aiello
President
The United States War Dogs Association

CAPSTONE PRESS
a capstone imprint

Edge Books are published by Capstone Press,
1710 Roe Crest Drive, North Mankato, Minnesota 56003
www.capstonepub.com

Copyright © 2014 by Capstone Press, a Capstone imprint. All rights reserved.
No part of this publication may be reproduced in whole or in part, or stored in a retrieval system, or transmitted in any form or by any means, electronic, mechanical, photocopying, recording, or otherwise, without written permission of the publisher.

Library of Congress Cataloging-in-Publication Data
Gagne, Tammy
Military dogs / by Tammy Gagne.
pages cm.—(Edge books: dogs on the job)
Includes index.
Audience: Grades 4 to 6.
ISBN 978-1-4765-0130-7 (library binding)
ISBN 978-1-4765-3386-5 (ebook PDF)
1. Dogs—War use—United States—Juvenile literature. I. Title.
UH100.G34 2014
355.4'24—dc23 2012051695

Editorial Credits
Brenda Haugen, editor; Kyle Grenz, designer; Marcie Spence, media researcher; Laura Manthe, production specialist

Photo Credits
Alamy Images: US Army Photo, 22, US Marines Photo, 21; AP Images: Corbis/AP Images, 12, Gregory Bull, 24; Connecticut Military Department, 8; Corbis: Bettmann, 10; Landov: HO/Reuters, 4; Newscom: Ahmad Masood/Reuters, cover, akg-Images, 13, Baz Ratner, 14, DoD/Sipa USA, 26, Erik De Castro/Reuters, 29, Everett Collection, 9, Finbarr O'Reilly/Reuters, 18, IDF/ChameleonsEye/Rafael Ben-Arl, 20, 28, Romeo Gacada/AFP/Getty Images, 6, SIPA USA, 5, Shamil Zhumatov/Reuters, 19, Yingling/MCT, 7; Shutterstock: gualtiero boffi, 16, Kachalkina Veronika, 15; Wikipedia: USGOV, 23

Printed in the United States of America in Stevens Point, Wisconsin.
032013 007227WZF13

Table of Contents

CHAPTER 1

Loyal and Brave Canines

American Navy SEAL Team 6 finished a dangerous mission on May 1, 2011. They killed Osama bin Laden, the Federal Bureau of Investigation's most wanted criminal. Bin Laden was responsible for planning the September 11, 2001, terrorist attacks on the United States, which killed nearly 3,000 people. The SEAL team found bin Laden in Abbottabad, Pakistan.

Military dogs are trained to search in any conditions, even darkness.

Some military dogs wear Doggles—goggles for dogs. They protect a dog's eyes from sunlight and flying debris.

The SEALs' dangerous mission got a lot of media attention. Although the Navy kept many details of the raid a secret, one team member's name was eventually revealed. But it wasn't a human team member's name. It was Cairo, the name of a highly trained military dog.

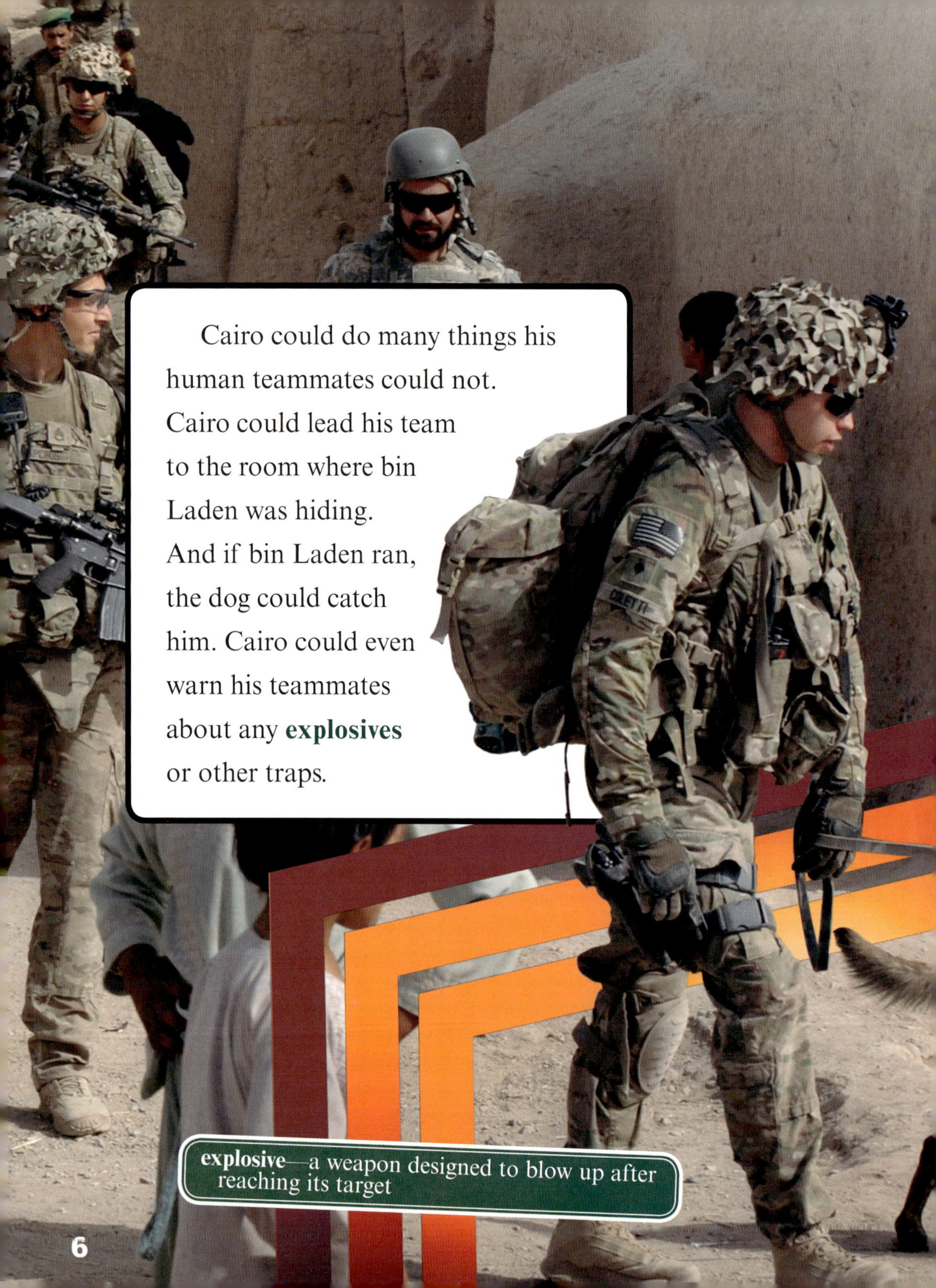

Cairo could do many things his human teammates could not. Cairo could lead his team to the room where bin Laden was hiding. And if bin Laden ran, the dog could catch him. Cairo could even warn his teammates about any **explosives** or other traps.

explosive—a weapon designed to blow up after reaching its target

Cairo wore a bulletproof vest. His vest also had a night-vision video camera. The camera allowed the SEALs to watch the live-action video as the dog moved from place to place. Cairo wore a tiny device in his ear. The device let Cairo's human partner whisper commands to the dog from several hundred yards away.

FACT

Cairo's K9 Storm Intruder vest cost more than $20,000.

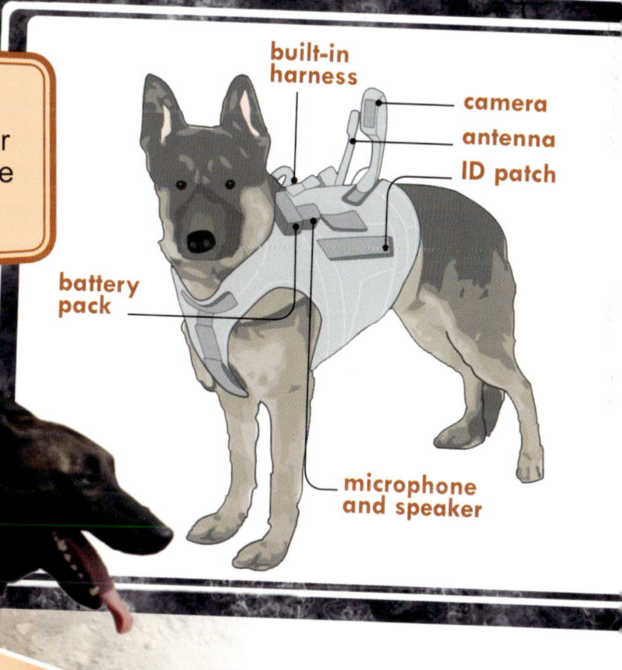

A soldier patrols with his dog in Afghanistan in 2011.

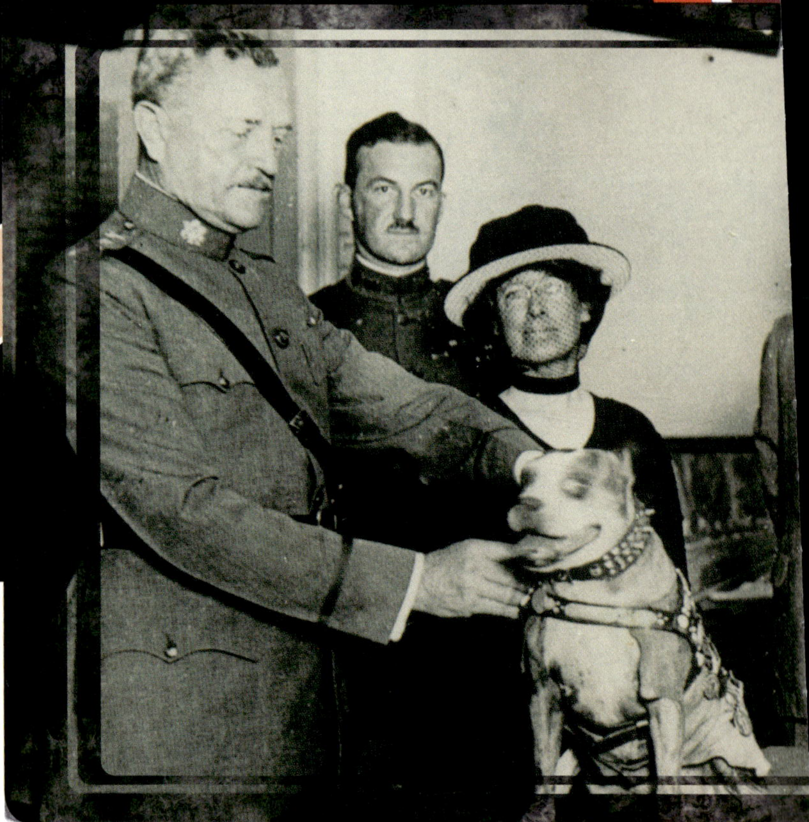

Stubby is awarded a medal by General John Pershing.

Dogs like Cairo have been working in militaries around the world for many years. Belgium, France, and Germany all used dogs in their militaries during World War I (1914–1918). Stubby was one of the first American **canine** soldiers. He was a bull terrier mix that Army Private J. Robert Conroy **smuggled** into France in 1918.

canine—to do with dogs

smuggle—to bring something or someone into or out of a country illegally

Stubby saved many lives during the war. He could hear incoming **artillery** shells long before human soldiers could. Stubby warned troops of the coming danger. He was the first dog to receive a military rank in the United States. The U.S. Army awarded him the title of sergeant. It remains the highest rank ever achieved by a dog.

A German shepherd keeps watch with a Coast Guardsman in 1942.

artillery—cannons and other large guns used during battles

CHAPTER 2

Getting Their Papers

American dog breeders began a training program for military dogs in 1942. Called the Dogs for Defense program, it trained dogs for the Army, Navy, and Coast Guard. The Marines also began using military dogs around this time. But the Marines chose and trained their own animals.

Super Dogs

Dogs for Defense was the United States' first military dog program. It still trains dogs today. But it hasn't been the only training program. The U.S. Army created the Super Dog Program in 1967. The program's goal was to breed and train the best military dogs in the world. By 1975 the Super Dog Program had produced 1,996 canine graduates.

At first only **purebred** dogs were allowed in military training programs. Many people thought that these dogs were smarter and more trustworthy than mixed breeds. Dogs for Defense required its dogs be at least 20 inches (51 centimeters) tall at the shoulder. The dogs could not be more than 5 years old. Military dogs also had to be good watchdogs. Dogs that were scared by gunfire or other loud noises would not make good canine soldiers.

FACT

The standard poodle was among the first breeds on the Dogs for Defense war dog list. Many poodles served as military guard dogs.

purebred—having parents of the same breed

Andy, a Doberman pinscher, served in Japan during World War II.

It soon became clear that certain breeds were better for use as military dogs. Dogs for Defense created its first list of war dogs in 1942. It included 32 breeds. By 1944 the list was shortened to five breeds. They were the Belgian sheep dog, Doberman pinscher, collie, German shepherd, and giant schnauzer. The Marines mainly used Doberman pinschers and German shepherds in their program.

FACT

Most military dogs are big. But some jobs call for smaller breeds. Jack Russell terriers sniff out bombs in submarines. These little dogs are the perfect size to fit in a sub's small spaces.

During World War II (1939–1945) it was hard to get certain purebred dogs. In time, Dogs for Defense changed its purebred rule. The group started training some mixed breeds. But the dogs still had to meet certain requirements. For example, light-colored dogs were not accepted because they could be seen too easily by enemies.

Today every branch of the U.S. military uses canine soldiers. These dogs guard military bases. They also protect human troops by warning them of approaching danger. Military dogs are trained to sniff out explosives too. They can even find the materials used to make dangerous weapons. Some are also trained to do search and rescue work. A new course even teaches dogs to find people who have planted bombs.

MPCs

Multi-purpose canines (MPCs) are part of military Special Operations Forces (SOF) teams, like the one that found bin Laden. MPCs are trained to jump out of airplanes with their handlers. MPCs also rappel with their handlers from helicopters. These dogs are not trained by the Dogs for Defense program. Instead, military contractors choose and train the animals that are used only by SOF.

Today training for military dogs lasts about four months. A **handler** is paired with each military dog. The handler learns how to control and work with the dog.

Handlers spend 93 days working with their dogs. The first 76 days are spent at Lackland Air Force Base in San Antonio, Texas. Both dogs and their handlers then travel to Yuma, Arizona, for another 17 days of training.

At the end of training, dogs are tested for **detection** and patrol. Only about half the dogs pass the tests. Dogs that pass go with their handlers to wherever they are needed.

handler—a person who trains or manages a dog for work or competition

detection—looking for certain items, such as bombs

CHAPTER 3

Reporting for Duty

Training can't prepare soldiers for everything they will face during war. Sometimes soldiers don't know what lies around the next corner. Canine soldiers face the same dangers as human troops.

Corporal Mike Dowling and his German shepherd Rex were part of the first Marine Corps K9 teams to see combat since the Vietnam War (1959–1975). The team was sent to Iraq during Operation Iraqi Freedom (2003–2011) in 2004.

German shepherds often make good military dogs.

FACT

Rex had been trained to sniff out weapons, ammunition, and bombs. Dowling's job was to lead the dog into the dangerous areas where these items lay hidden.

While camping in an empty warehouse one night, Dowling and Rex came under an enemy **mortar** attack. Dowling used his body to shield Rex. A fellow Marine tried to take cover in a nearby Humvee. He was killed when the vehicle took a direct hit. Rex and his handler saw many other deaths as they endured the night.

Dowling and Rex came home safely after their tour in Iraq. They saved many lives together. Rex served two more tours in Iraq with a new handler.

mortar—a short cannon that fires shells or rockets high in the air

FACT

Organizations such as the Humane Society of the United States help military dogs by providing them with special cooling vests. Temperatures in the Middle East can reach 130 degrees Fahrenheit (54 degrees Celsius).

Military dogs must have incredible focus on the job. They cannot be distracted by birds or other wildlife. They also cannot be frightened by loud noises, such as gunshots or explosions.

The day-to-day work the dogs do can be rather boring. But this can change at any moment. A handler may guide the dog from one place to another. Along the way the dog sniffs for guns or explosives. The animal's job is to find these dangers before they can harm anyone. The team might not find anything suspicious for some time.

Other dogs stay in one spot, guarding checkpoints. These dogs sniff cars before human soldiers allow them to pass through certain areas. Again, the dog is looking for threats to American soldiers. Days might pass without any problems.

War Dog

Lieutenant Jay Kopelman found a tiny puppy while serving in Fallujah, Iraq, during Operation Iraqi Freedom. He named the dog Lava. Kopelman knew that keeping a stray dog was not allowed. But for Kopelman and his fellow Marines, Lava was something normal in a place where nothing else seemed normal at all.

When it came time to move on, Kopelman did not want to leave Lava behind. But the dog could not travel to the United States without a health certificate and shots from a veterinarian. And no military veterinarians were willing to examine a civilian dog.

Still, Kopelman refused to give up. With the help of National Public Radio journalist Anne Garrels and others, he finally got Lava to the United States. The dog now has a home with Kopelman and his family.

When danger appears, the dog's job becomes anything but dull. Canine teams can encounter steady gunfire. They have no guarantee that they will make it out alive.

FACT

During World War I the Red Cross trained dogs to locate people who were hurt. These dogs found hundreds of wounded soldiers. Many times the dogs even dragged unconscious men to safety.

Sometimes unit members get separated during battles. When this happens, military dogs can help reunite them by using their sense of smell. Dogs trained in search and rescue can also find injured soldiers who are lost among rubble.

The bonds between military dogs and their handlers become very strong. A handler and dog may spend years together. Many dogs save the lives of human soldiers. Sometimes the dogs die saving soldiers. At other times handlers may risk their lives to save their fellow soldiers, including their dogs. This was the case of Staff Sergeant Robert Hartsock.

the U.S. Army Medal of Honor

The United States was fighting the Vietnam War when enemies attacked Hartsock's camp. During the attack Hartsock threw himself on an explosive to save his fellow troops. He continued to hold off the enemy even though he was badly hurt from the explosion. The attack lasted for more than nine hours. In the end Hartsock died of his wounds. The lives he saved that day included human and canine soldiers, including his German shepherd, Duke. Hartsock became the only dog handler to receive the Medal of Honor for his actions during the Vietnam War.

CHAPTER 4

Canine Veterans

Being a military dog is hard work. When canine soldiers get older, their bodies can no longer perform the way they did when they were young. Many military dogs retire around the age of 10. Some handlers adopt their dogs. Other dogs are adopted by **civilian** families. Finding the right match for each veteran dog is important. The dogs have had a lot of training, but they have not lived in a home.

civilian—a person who is not in the military

Most ex-military dogs do fine in civilian homes after they get used to their new surroundings. Many of them need extra training for civilian life. This begins with **socializing** them to other animals. Military dogs are not allowed much contact with other animals during their years of service. It is also important to keep these dogs as active as possible. They will likely become bored and frustrated if they do not have something to do.

Air Force Staff Sergeant James Bailey is among the handlers to adopt their dogs. His Belgian Malinois Robby lives with him in Virginia. Robby shares his new home and fenced yard with a 65-pound (29-kg) dog named Gunner. Bailey has said that Robby kept him safe in Iraq. Now he is giving something back to Robby.

socialize—to train to get along with people and other dogs

Organizations such as Military Working Dog Adoptions help find homes for retired military dogs. Sometimes these groups even save the dogs' lives. This was the case with Dexter.

Dexter was a valuable military service dog. He saved up to 1,000 lives at Abu Ghraib in Iraq in 2004 by finding explosives on a garbage truck. But as he aged, Dexter began suffering from hip problems. The military decided to **euthanize** him. But Dexter's handler, Kathleen Ellison, fought hard against this decision. She wanted to adopt him, but she needed the military's permission.

Congressmen Maurice D. Hinchey and Walter Jones, along with others, came to Ellison's aid. Ellison was finally able to take Dexter home. On December 29, 2008, Dexter came back to the United States for the first time in 10 years.

euthanize—to put an animal to death by injecting it with a substance that stops its breathing or heartbeat

Driven by loyalty to their handlers, military dogs work long and hard for their countries. The dogs spend most of their lives risking their well-being for the safety of others.

They are true military heroes.

Canine Hero

The American Humane Association honors working dogs with its Hero Dog Awards. This annual event pays tribute to canine bravery. In 2011 the winning military dog was a Dutch shepherd named Bino. He spent 14 months in Iraq. But this was just one of the many jobs he has had. He had also worked almost 11 years as a patrol dog at Fort Gordon, Georgia. Bino also served on special missions with the U.S. Border Patrol.

After he retired from the military and Border Patrol, Bino had another job. He helped train service dogs. These animals help people with disabilities. They are also trained to let someone know if their owners need emergency medical treatment.

Glossary

artillery (ar-TIL-uh-ree)—cannons and other large guns used during battles

canine (KAY-nyn)—to do with dogs

civilian (si-VIL-yuhn)—a person who is not in the military

detection (dee-TEK-shuhn)—looking for certain items, such as bombs

euthanize (YOO-thuh-nyz)—to put an animal to death by injecting it with a substance that stops its breathing or heartbeat

explosive (ik-SPLOH-siv)—a weapon designed to blow up after reaching its target

handler (HAND-lur)—a person who trains or manages a dog for work or competition

mortar (MOR-tur)—a short cannon that fires shells or rockets high in the air

purebred (PYOOR-bred)—having parents of the same breed

smuggle (SMUHG-uhl)—to bring something or someone into or out of a country illegally

socialize (SOH-shuh-lize)—to train to get along with people and other dogs

Read More

Gagne, Tammy. *German Shepherds.* All about Dogs. Mankato, Minn.: Capstone Press, 2009.

Kadohata, Cynthia. *Cracker! The Best Dog in Vietnam.* New York: Atheneum Books for Young Readers, 2007.

Ruffin, Frances E. *Military Dogs.* New York: Bearport Pub., 2007.

Internet Sites

FactHound offers a safe, fun way to find Internet sites related to this book. All of the sites on FactHound have been researched by our staff.

Here's all you do:

Visit *www.facthound.com*

Type in this code: 9781476501307

Super-cool stuff!

Check out projects, games and lots more at **www.capstonekids.com**

Index